# My Fellow Americans,

*it's cool...
to speak like you've
been to school!*

#1 Speech & Voice Make-Over Manual Helping Young African Americans, Latino Americans, Hip Hop Lovers, & Others Get a Job Faster!

By: Dr. Bernadette Anderson

© 2009 Dr. Bernadette Anderson
Revised Copy in Second Printing 2010

My Fellow Americans… It's Cool to Speak Like You've Been to School

©2009 Bernadette Anderson

All rights reserved. This book is protected by the copyright laws of the United States of America and may not be copied, printed, reproduced, stored in a retrieval system, or transmitted, in any form, or by any means, mechanical, electronic, or otherwise without the prior written consent of the publisher.

   Published by: The Speech Excel Center®, Inc.
                         P.O. Box 16744
                         Chicago, IL 60616
"For People Who Value Good Communication Skills"®

ISBN 978-0-615-30110-5

Publisher's Note

The information provided in this book to improve voice quality is not intended to be a substitute for the direct therapeutic services of a state-licensed, ASHA (American Speech-Language-Hearing Association) Certified Speech-Language Pathologist. Every reader is advised to carefully review and understand the ideas and suggested tips on how to project the voice and improve voice quality first. Second, each reader is advised to seek the advice of a qualified medical professional before implementing the vocal tips, especially if any voice-related problems are suspected. The publisher and editor disclaim all liability (including any damages, injuries, or losses) resulting from the use of information contained in this book.

Graphic Design by Stacy Drake

Table of Contents

Preface 2
DEDICATION 3
Introduction 4
Placing S on 3rd Person Singular Verbs 7
Using Am, Is Are, to Replace Be 13
Asking Questions 21
Adding S for Possession 31
Future Perfect Tense: Will have vs Be Done 38
About Regular Verbs 39
Exercises to Use Future Perfect Tense 42
What is Present Perfect Tense? 46
About Irregular Verbs 46
List of Regular Verbs 49
List of Irregular Verbs 51
Present Perfect Tense 55
Exercises to Use Present Perfect Tense 56
Ain't Nobody, Cain't Nobody, Don't Nobody, Won't Nobody 60
PRONUNCIATION TIPS 78
    ASK 78
    ASKED 79
    STR 80
    SCR or SKR 80
    The Th Sounds 81
8 Rules to Breath Control for Voice Control 84
The Harsh Voice and How to Change It 85
The Nasal Voice and How to Change It 86
IN CONCLUSION 87
The "Link" Continues 89
ABOUT THE AUTHOR 90

My Fellow Americans...It's Cool to Speak Like You've Been to School
© 2009 by Bernadette Anderson, Ph.D., All Rights Reserved

Preface

On January 20, 2009, I watched my television screen with intense focus, excitement, and thanksgiving to God, as my former instructor, Barack Hussein Obama, became the 44th President of the United States. My mind flashed back eleven years ago to January 1998, when Obama stood before twenty-four of us concerned citizens who had enrolled in a 12-week workshop series, titled "Leadership in the Community," a course which Obama helped develop with another community leader. I remembered two unique aspects about Obama. The first was the question he posed to us: "What is power?" Since we had gained the answer during the previous session, we were able to respond confidently: "Power is Organized People and Organized Money!" Obama grinned from ear to ear, obviously pleased with the way we had answered him. The second unique aspect about him was the personal news he shared with us, as he announced, "I am so happy because my wife and I are expecting our first child." We applauded his joy.

On the night of the Presidential Inaugural Balls, I cried as Beyonce tearfully, beautifully and passionately sang the romantic song, "At Last," while President Obama and First Lady Michelle danced lovingly and triumphantly to the song. In an interview right after she sang, Beyonce broke down in tears, as she expressed her sentiments (and, no doubt, those of millions) regarding Obama's winning the Presidency: "He makes me want to be *smarter*." I hope that all who read and *use* My Fellow Americans: It's Cool to Speak Like You've Been to School will *feel smarter* too.

Bernadette Anderson, Ph.D.

DEDICATION

This book is dedicated to my beloved mother, Mrs. Ernestine Anderson, who suggested to me several years ago: "Bernie (a name term of endearment reserved for those who have known me ever since I was a child, or since they were children), why don't you write a book that shows a speaker when to say <u>seen</u> and when to say <u>saw</u>, because it is so confusing when you don't know." Finally, after producing training manuals, cassettes and CD's to help improve the speaking skills of American speakers in general, I have written a book that is focused on specific aspects of grammar, and pronunciation unique to speakers of African American English dialect.

My Fellow Americans...It's Cool to Speak Like You've Been to School

By Dr. Bernadette Anderson

In business, whether you are speaking over the telephone, during an interview by television or radio, in a small or large group, or face to face, you want your listeners' attention to be on *your message*, not on what listeners perceive to be *misuse of grammar* or *mispronunciation* of words.

It's a New Day. We have the first African American President of the United States, Barack Hussein Obama, whose speech is extraordinarily eloquent, yet down to earth, to captivate, motivate and mobilize millions of listeners: young, middle-aged, and old; black, brown, yellow and white; Christians, Muslims, Hindus, and Jews; educated and non educated, wealthy and non-wealthy.

Having spent many years training non-native medical and business professionals in ways to reduce their accents, so that they could be understood better by their patients, customers and colleagues, I remember and laugh out loud at some of the responses of astonishment shown by my clients when they actually met me. The most poignant was Dr. Haiku (fake name), head of nuclear medicine at a hospital in Osaka, Japan, who had come to the Northwestern University Medical School in Chicago as an exchange physician, who found me in the Yellow Pages. After speaking with me for only two minutes, he stated emphatically, "I want to come see you now! I want to come see you now!" I adjusted my schedule to accommodate him, and when Dr. Haiku knocked at the door of my Chicago Downtown office, I opened the door and greeted him. He then said, "I want to see Dr. Anderson." I assured him, "I *am* Dr. Anderson." We went through this volley three times, until Dr. Haiku finally understood that "the voice" on the phone belonged to me, an African American woman. He then said, "I want *only* Standard American English" in staccato cadence.

Matching his cadence, I said, "Don't worry, Dr. Haiku. You will be trained in *only* Standard American English." As I worked with him to alter his speech rhythm, intonation, articulation, and pronunciation, I watched his face glow with pleasure, as he saw and heard the changes in his accent on the video training tapes used during our sessions.

I also laugh when I recall how the husband of my Korean female client fell backward out of the office door and nearly landed on the floor of a downtown motel which the couple owned. The husband, also Korean, had decided to change his plans, return to the office unexpectedly, and surprise both his wife and her new "English Pronunciation Teacher." Both husband and wife had been very surprised to learn that the smooth, clear voice and crisp speech they had heard via phone belonged to me, an African American woman. Nevertheless, they were elated by her changed accent.

Probably the most memorable of all my non-native clients was Dr. Lertsbapa (fake name), a renowned surgeon who, upon arriving at my downtown office, kept looking over my head for whom he envisioned to be "Dr. Anderson." I assured him twice with a smile that I was truly Dr. Anderson. After being seated comfortably in my administrative office, Dr. Lertsbapa said, "But you <u>deceived</u> me!" Laughing, I asked him, "How did I *deceive* you?" He said, *"Your first name,* Bernadette, is *French.* Your last name, Anderson, is *Swedish."* He said he expected to see a *white, blonde,* blue-eyed speech trainer. We both laughed at his perceptions. I explained to him that I had learned to speak five languages over the years, and that I loved listening to different accents and imitating them. We both agreed that the more important aspect of communication was the *"content"* of the message, rather than the *imprecision* of the *tongue,* which could *muddle the message, divert* the attention of the listeners, and *rob* the speaker of the impact the message was intended to achieve. We agreed that the main language, rather than a *dialect* of it, is expected in business.

A *dialect* is a variation of a language, which often allows a listener to identify a speaker's origin, and race. Standard American English, while considered the language of business in America, is a *dialect* of English. After all, English was not created in America, but rather, in England. Many Americans speak English in ways that allow them to be identified racially; one variation of spoken American English is often called African American English Dialect (AAED), (also called

Black English Dialect and Ebonics) , which is governed by rules and identified by specific features, among which include: (1) the absence of the "S" at the end of <u>verbs </u>in the <u>present tense </u>with a <u>third person subject;</u> (2) use of the verb <u>Be</u> followed by a descriptor, such as happy, sad, etc., or in front of a <u>verb+ing phrase</u>; (3) use of the phrase "Be Done" before a verb for future perfect tense; (4) Subject-Led questions; and (5) specific word pronunciations.

The infectious love for hip hop, especially rapping, which typically contains elements of African American English dialect, has influenced the speech patterns of the young globally to the extent that many of them who are *not* African Americans use African American English dialect when communicating with others.

There is *nothing wrong* with the use of African American English Dialect. I grew up hearing and speaking it. I continue to use it with family members and friends, because use of it engenders depth of meaning and feelings of love and connection. However, in business interactions I use Standard American English to ensure that my listeners' attention is on the content of my message, not on any *perceived* errors in grammar or pronunciation.

Having appeared as a guest on the Oprah Winfrey Show in 1987 and the Geraldo Rivera Show in 1997 on the topics of "Black English Dialect" and "Ebonics," respectively, I have encouraged many African Americans to be multi-dialectal, having the ability to "flip the switch" verbally in order to speak effectively in whatever speaking situation they find themselves. I strongly suggest using Standard American English during those more formal occasions, i.e., job interviews, meetings with supervisors, consultations with business associates, customers, etc., when you want your listeners to pay close attention to *what* you say, rather than *how* you say it. Once the basics are learned, it's easy to "flip the switch."

Now, rather than bog you down with boring grammar rules, I will give you a brief <u>Discussion </u>of the speech changes you will be making and <u>POINTS</u> to <u>REMEMBER</u>. Use these points to make your speech sound more "business appropriate."

1. Discussion: Knowing When to Place an "S" on Verbs. This has to do with the Third Person Singular Subject and Present Tense Verb. The third person singular subject refers to one person (neither you nor I), one place, or one thing. Think of a verb as anything you can do. Think of present tense as routine tense, or time, when something occurs regularly, or on a routine basis.

A speaker of African American English Dialect (AAED) might say:

    John work hard.   OR   He work hard.

    Mary eat corn.   OR   She eat corn.

    The music sound loud. OR It sound loud.

POINT #1..... REMEMBER: NO MAN IS AN ISLAND; EVERYONE NEEDS...

Someone

Just take the "S" from the word "Someone" and attach it to the ends of work, eat, and sound above, so that you switch the sentences to Standard American English, as shown below. Consequently, each, subject---John, Mary, and music--will have "Someone" after the "S" has been-attached to the verb.

Standard American English

Ex.   John works hard.   OR   He works hard.

      Mary eats corn.   OR   She eats corn.

      The music sounds loud. OR It sounds loud.

Change the African American English Dialect sentences below to Standard American English ones by placing an S on verbs in the present, or routine tense. Afterwards, check your answers against the KEY, which follows.

1. Mary go to work early.

___

2. Bill always forget his umbrella.

___

3. She make more money than anybody we know.

___

4. Timothy bring two sandwiches to work every day.

___

5. Mr. and Mrs. Smith live on Elm Street.

___

(No changes are needed, because the Smiths have Someone in each other.)

6. Ernestine grow beautiful flowers.

___

7. The nurse give the patients their medicine.

___

8. Philip spend his summers on St. Helena Island.

___

9. The lab report look like a ransom note.

___

10. Charlotte eat right, exercise, and look great.

___

11. Fredericka read day and night

12. The door open every time.

13. Sandra believe that anything is possible.

14. Von love her husband and family.

15. Bravo, the dog, enjoy taking walks.

16. The phone ring off the hook.

17. The mail usually arrive at 1:00 p.m.

18. Sheila take a longer lunch break than she should.

19. When Bill throw a party, everybody come.

20. Robert stand tall and say what he think.

21. Barbara do hair on Wednesdays and Fridays.

22. Her clients say she <u>do</u> a better job than anyone else.

_____

23. President Barack Obama <u>speak</u> with solid confidence.

_____

24. He <u>make</u> us feel hopeful.

_____

25. Jonathan Green <u>paint</u> the most beautiful images.

_____

KEY

(To the Exercise above on Third Person, Singular Subject, in the **Present** or **Routine** Tense)

1. GOES
2. FORGETS
3. MAKES
4. BRINGS
5. LIVE
6. GROWS
7. GIVES
8. SPENDS
9. LOOKS
10. EATS, EXERCISES, LOOKS
11. READS
12. OPENS
13. BELIEVES
14. LOVES
15. ENJOYS
16. RINGS
17. ARRIVES
18. TAKES
19. THROWS, COMES

20. STANDS, SAYS, THINKS

21. DOES

22. DOES

23. SPEAKS

24. MAKES

25. PAINTS

2. Discussion: Knowing When to Use the Verbs Am, Are, and Is in the Present, or Routine, Tense to Replace the Verb Be. Many speakers of African American English dialect use the verb Be, rather than Am, Are, or Is before a descriptor, such as happy, scared, etc., before a gerund (verb+ing), such as running, coughing, etc., or before a locator, i.e., a preposition, such as in, on, etc.

The Verb Be is used in this way to indicate consistency and reliability.

For example, a speaker of African American English Dialect (AAED) might say:

    I be happy when I go shopping.

    You be running faster than Joe.

    Karen be upstairs in her room by 6:00 p.m.

In each sentence the subject (I, You, Karen) gives the impression that the action is committed on a consistent basis.

Changing the same sentences to Standard American English results in:

    I am happy when I go shopping.

    You are running faster than Joe.

    Karen is upstairs in her room by 6:00 p.m.

NOTE:

When changing an African American English Dialect sentence containing the verb Be followed by a gerund (verb+ing), eg., "be laughing," you can make the change to Standard American English by eliminating the verb Be and the ing at the end of the second verb.

Example:

African American English Dialect:

> I be laughing when I watch old comedies.

Change it to Standard American English:

> I laugh when I watch old comedies.

You might recall hearing your English teacher say:

"The forms of the verb To Be in the Present (or Routine) Tense with Singular (one) Pronoun Subjects in Standard American English are:

Singular Pronouns	Examples:
Am with 1st Person – I	I am happy.
Are with 2nd Person, -- You	You are happy.
Is with 3rd Person – He, She, It	He, She or It is happy.

The same English teacher might have said also:

"The forms of the verb To Be in the Present (or Routine) Tense with Plural (more than one) Pronoun Subjects in Standard American English are: are, are, are.

Plural Pronouns	Examples:
Are with 1st Person – We	We are happy.
Are with 2nd Person – You	You are happy.
Are with 3rd Person – They	They are happy.

As the examples above show, in Standard American English the forms (or spellings) of the verb To Be are Am, Are and Is for Singular Pronoun Subjects and Are for Plural Pronoun Subjects.

Perhaps you are asking: "If a verb is 'anything you can do,' what makes To Be a verb?" A simple answer to this question is: "To be means To exist." Do you exist? Of course, you exist; therefore, you are.

During most of this Discussion I have used Pronouns in the sentences. To avoid any confusion that could arise regarding the use of a Noun or Pronoun, bear in mind that a Noun is a Name of a person, place or thing, and a Pronoun is a substitute for a Noun. The prefix Pro = in place of; so a Pronoun is used "in place of" a Noun.

POINT #2......... REMEMBER: Use the Present Tense Forms of the verb To Be--Am, Is, or Are—with the Descriptor of a Subject, such as tired, a Gerund (VERB+ING), or Locator, i.e., a PREPOSITION.

Change the African American English Dialect sentences which follow to Standard American English ones by replacing the verb Be with Am, Is, or Are, or by using the major verb of the gerund (verb +ing) with or without S. Afterwards, check your answers against the KEY, which follows.

Exercises to Replace Be with Am, Is, Are

1. Bob and Anna usually <u>be</u> alone at night.

   _____

2. Those teachers <u>be</u> in a hurry to go home.

   _____

3. Who <u>be</u> at the team meeting on Saturday?

   _____

4. You know I <u>be</u> mad when they don't show up.

   _____

5. The traffic <u>be</u> heavy from morning to night.

   _____

6. Jackie and Edith <u>be</u> on time for work.

   _____

7. Who <u>be</u> <u>watching</u> the kids when you <u>be</u> at work?

   _____

8. Whoever <u>be</u> <u>making</u> all that noise should stop it.

   _____

9. When I <u>don't</u> <u>be</u> busy, I don't mind helping out.

   _____

10. Some of the students <u>be</u> quiet, but some <u>be</u> talking.

___

11. When Tom <u>be</u> at work, Judy <u>be</u> babysitting.

___

12. How many contestants <u>be</u> on the stage at once?

___

13. Those security guards <u>be</u> earning their money.

___

14. The people <u>be</u> <u>shouting</u> as their pastor <u>be</u> preaching.

___

15. Gina and Pat <u>be</u> the only cousins who go on trips.

___

16. I do not go to that store because Jack <u>be</u> there.

___

17. People <u>be</u> <u>fixing</u> a lot of food for the Super Bowl.

___

18. Bob <u>be playing</u> in class, while his teacher <u>be</u> watching him.

___

19. Some businesses <u>be</u> laying off employees.

___

20. When the boys <u>be</u> outside, they <u>be</u> running around.

_____

21. If you <u>be</u> with the wrong crowd, you act like them.

_____

22. You <u>be</u> <u>feeling</u> good when you get compliments.

_____

23. I <u>be</u> <u>waiting</u> all day for the mailman to come.

_____

24. We <u>be</u> <u>working</u> hard, while they <u>be taking</u> it easy.

_____

25. When you <u>be</u> prepared, you <u>be</u> equipped for success.

_____

KEY

(To the Exercises above on Replacing the Verb <u>Be</u> in African American English dialect in Present Tense).

1. ARE

2. ARE

3. IS

4. AM

5. IS

6. ARE

7. ARE WATCHING, ARE

8. IS MAKING

9. AM NOT

10. ARE, ARE

11. IS, IS

12. ARE

14. ARE SHOUTING, IS PREACHING

15. ARE

16. IS

17. ARE FIXING

18. IS PLAYING OR PLAYS, IS WATCHING OR WATCHES

19. ARE

20. ARE, ARE

21. ARE

22. ARE FEELING OR FEEL

23. AM WAITING OR WAIT

24. ARE WORKING OR WORK, ARE TAKING OR TAKE

25. ARE, ARE

3. Discussion: Knowing How to Ask a Question by <u>Leading</u> with the <u>Question Word</u> (Who, What, Which, Where, When, Why, How), followed by the <u>Verb</u> and then the <u>Subject</u>. Many speakers of African American English Dialect do just the <u>Opposite</u> with the <u>Order</u> of <u>Verb</u> and <u>Subject</u>. That is, they <u>Lead</u> with the <u>Subject</u> and then <u>Follow</u> with the <u>Verb</u> or <u>Verb Phrase</u>. The following is a very popular question style in <u>African American</u> <u>English</u> <u>Dialect</u> (or AAED):

"Why <u>You Didn't Come</u> to my party?"

Notice that the <u>Subject</u>, <u>You</u>, is mentioned *BEFORE* the <u>Verb Phrase,</u> *Didn't Come* in AAED. Also notice that if the <u>Question Word</u>, "Why," were removed, the speaker would be making a statement:

"<u>You</u> <u>Didn't Come</u> to my party."

If you "Flip the Switch," or "Change the word order," by leading with the <u>first word</u>, "Didn't," in the verb phrase, you form the <u>Standard American English question</u>:

"Why <u>Didn't</u> You <u>Come</u> to my party?"

This time if the Question Word, "Why," were removed, the speaker would still be asking a question:

"Didn't You Come to my party?"

When in doubt about whether you are going to ask a question in Standard American English, or SAE, simply *remove* the Question Word (Who, What, Which, Where, When, Why, How) mentally, and say to yourself the rest of the question you want to ask, and if the rest of the question sounds like a statement, rather than a question, then you are asking your question in African American English

Dialect, or AAED, NOT in Standard American English, or SAE, which is more accepted in business. Try using this tip on the following four questions and identify the type of question as one in SAE or AAED by writing SAE or AAED on the short lines that follow:

1. Why your manager didn't call you sooner? _____

2. When did your manager call Bob Klinker? _____

3. How Judy mistook your report for mine? _____

4. Where your son Jeffery took his date for dinner? ____

(The quick answers are AAED, SAE AAED, AAED.)

Often in AAED, the verb, or part of a verb phrase, is omitted, as in:

"Where Shawna?" or "Where Shawna at?"

Convert this AAED question to one in Standard American English by inserting the appropriate form of the verb To Be (Am, Is, Are) before Shawna:

"Where Is Shawna?"

I advise you to avoid ending questions with prepositions, such as in, at or on, as in "Where is Shawna at?" whenever you can do so smoothly, or without feeling "verbally clumsy," because according to the rules of Standard American English grammar, it is still more acceptable to ask a question without saying a preposition at the end. In "Where is Shawna at?" adding the locator, or preposition, "AT" does not add value to the question, so remove it, and simply say:

"Where is Shawna?"

POINT #3........ REMEMBER: In Standard American English questions, the question word (who, what, which, where, when, why how) comes first, followed by the main verb or the first word in the main verb phrase, which is followed by the subject; and the remainder of the main verb phrase follows.

Change the following African American English Dialect questions into Standard American English ones. Write your sentences on the lines provided, and say the questions out loud, so that you may <u>become</u> <u>more</u> <u>accustomed</u> to hearing yourself ask questions in Standard American English. Then check your answers against the KEY, which follows.

Exercises to Ask Questions in Standard American English

1. Where Jonathan and Shawna at?

2. Who your friend in the red and gold dress?

3. What the principal going to do to inspire the students?

4. When you first noticed the dog walking toward Billy?

5. Why he turned around so suddenly?

6. How Mr. Tibbs knew where to find us?

7. Why Ms. Tano always think her students right?

8. How the Coach be knowing who leave food in the gym?

9. How you managed to stay calm in that awful situation?

10. When the landlord told you to vacate the apartment?

11. How many times you advised the employees to save?

12. Ellen, why you didn't warn me about that other guy?

13. Who Lindsey married after his third divorce?

14. What kind of dog Brenda want to rescue now?

15. Which pain killers Monica took for her headache?

16. When Carla and Matthew registered to vote?

17. Where they put the rest of my furniture?

18. Why your skirts be so tight?

19. When you first learned about the strike?

20. Which outfit Barbara didn't like?

21. How you broke your foot?

22. Why they didn't inform the manager about the incident?

23. Where you thought you dropped the keys?

24. How I'm supposed to remember all those numbers?

25. Why the drummers in the band didn't wear shirts?

26. Why the police chief didn't give you that award?

27. How Bruce was supposed to feed his kids with no job?

28. Where the football coach positioned his best players?

29. Where they put the rest of my furniture?

30. Where Jake took Mary for her birthday celebration?

31. Who you thought sent the threatening e-mail?

32. Who know where Bob be taking Alice for lunch?

33. What we supposed to use for uniforms?

34. Where those employees sat when they harassed her?

35. How Harry finished his work in less than an hour?

36. Which speaker you thought was the most convincing?

37. How old the boy said he was when he texted you?

38. Where the relatives held a family reunion last year?

39. How she thought she could take care of twelve babies?

40. Which woman Richard asked to go out with him?

41. How much money Tony paid Harry to wash his car?

42. When Harry discovered he was washing the wrong car?

43. What your name is?

44. When your birthday is?

45. What kind of work you do?

46. Why you don't like to answer questions?

47. How your friends kept the party a secret for so long?

48. Where you bought your coats for so little money?

49. When you finished editing the book for Dennis?

50. In 1998 how Obama defined power?

(For the answer to this question, read the "Preface.")

KEY

(To the Exercises above on changing word order and verb forms to ask questions in Standard American English-SAE)

1. Where <u>are</u> Jonathan and Shawna?
2. Who <u>is</u> your friend in the red and gold dress?
3. What <u>is</u> the Principal <u>going</u> to do to inspire the students?
4. When <u>did</u> you first <u>notice</u> the dog walking toward Billy?
5. Why <u>did</u> he <u>turn</u> around so suddenly?
6. How <u>did</u> Mr. Tibbs <u>know</u> where to find us?
7. Why <u>does</u> Ms. Tano always <u>think</u> her students <u>are</u> right?
8. How <u>does</u> the Coach know who <u>leaves</u> food in the gym?
9. How <u>did</u> you <u>manage</u> to stay calm in that awful situation?
10. When <u>did</u> the landlord <u>tell</u> you to vacate the apartment?
11. How many times <u>did</u> you <u>advise</u> the employees to save?
12. Ellen, why <u>didn't</u> you <u>warn</u> me about that other guy?
13. Who <u>did</u> Lindsey <u>marry</u> after his third divorce?
14. What kind of dog <u>does</u> Brenda <u>want</u> to rescue now?
15. Which pain killers <u>did</u> Monica <u>take</u> for her headache?
16. When <u>did</u> Carla and Matthew <u>register</u> to vote?
17. Where <u>did</u> they <u>put</u> the rest of my furniture?
18. Why <u>are</u> your skirts so tight?
19. When <u>did</u> you first <u>learn</u> about the strike?

20. Which outfit didn't Barbara like?

21. How did you break your foot?

22. Why didn't they inform the manager about the incident?

23. Where did you think you dropped the keys.

24. How am I supposed to remember all those numbers?

25. Why didn't the drummers in the band wear shirts?

26. Why didn't the police chief give you that award?

27. How was Bruce supposed to feed his kids with no job?

28. Where did the football coach position his best players?

29. Where did they put the rest of my furniture?

30. Where did Jake take Mary for her birthday celebration?

31. Who did you think sent the threatening e-mail?

32. Who knows where Bob takes Alice for lunch?

33. What are we supposed to use for uniforms?

34. Where did those employees sit when they harassed her?

35. How did Harry finish his work in less than an hour?

36. Which speaker did you think was the most convincing?

37. How old did the boy say he was when he texted you?

38. Where did the relatives hold a family reunion last year?

39. How did she think she could take care of twelve babies?

40. Which woman did Richard ask to go out with him?

41. How much money did Tony pay Harry to wash his car?

42. When <u>did</u> Harry <u>discover</u> he was washing the wrong car?

43. What <u>is</u> your name?

44. When <u>is</u> your birthday?

45. What kind of work <u>do</u> you <u>do</u>?

46. Why <u>don't</u> you <u>like</u> to answer questions?

47. How <u>did</u> your friends <u>keep</u> the party a secret for so long?

48. Where <u>did</u> you <u>buy</u> your coats for so little money?

49. When <u>did</u> you <u>finish</u> editing the book for Dennis?

50. In 1998 how <u>did</u> Obama <u>define</u> power?

(For the answer to this question, read the "Preface.")

4. Discussion: Knowing when to add the <u>S</u> sound to the end of a <u>spoken</u> noun or <u>apostrophe S</u> (' S) to the end of a <u>written</u> noun to show <u>possession</u>, or <u>ownership</u>. Many speakers of African American English Dialect (AAED) show possession by saying the noun <u>without</u> the <u>S</u> sound at the end of a spoken noun preceding the name of whatever is being possessed.

For example, a speaker of African American English Dialect (AAED) might say:

    Marion house on the southwest corner.

    Leonard car in the shop.

    Stewart painting won first place in the contest.

    Sylvia baby name Nakia.

In each sentence the noun is spoken before the name it possesses. Changing the AAED sentences above into SAE sentences results in:

    Marion'<u>s</u> house <u>is</u> on the southwest corner.

    Leonard'<u>s</u> car <u>is</u> in the shop.

    Stewart'<u>s</u> painting won first place in the contest.

    Sylvia'<u>s</u> baby'<u>s</u> name <u>is</u> Nakia.

Often African American English Dialect (AAED) speakers use the singular objective pronoun – <u>him</u>, rather than the singular possessive pronoun – <u>his</u>, before gerunds (verbs ending in <u>ing</u>), as follows:

Ex: I heard stories about <u>him</u> walking for miles.

Some African American English Dialect (AAED) speakers use the plural nominative (nom=name) pronoun – <u>they</u>, rather than the plural possessive pronoun – <u>their</u>, before nouns to show possession, as follows:

Ex: The neighbors want <u>they</u> voices to be heard.

Changing the same sentences to Standard American English (SAE) results in:

> I heard stories about <u>his</u> walking for miles.

> The neighbors want <u>their</u> voices to be heard.

Some AAED speakers add S to the end of <u>mine</u> to show possession, as follows:

Ex: Bob lost his money and <u>mines</u>.

Changing the same sentence to SAE would result in: Bob lost his money and <u>mine</u>.

The following are the Possessive Pronouns in <u>SAE</u>

	Singular Possessive	Plural Possessive
1st	My (See my hair.)	Our (It's our house)
	Mine (That's mine.)	Ours (It is ours.)
	NEVER say "That's mine<u>s</u>."	
2nd	Your, yours	Your, yours
3rd	His	Their, theirs
	Her, hers	
	Its	

The following are the <u>Objective</u> <u>Pronouns</u> in <u>SAE</u>

	Singular Objective	Plural Objective
1st	Me	Us
2nd	You	You
3rd	Him, Her, It	Them

Things are done <u>to</u> or <u>for</u> <u>objects</u>, so things are done <u>to</u> or <u>for</u> Objective Pronouns.

Ex: Bob spoke to me, to you (one person), to him, to her, to it, to us, to you (more than one person), and to them.

POINT #4......REMEMBER: In Standard American English use the possessive pronoun (my, your-singular, his, her, its, our, your-plural, their), rather than the objective pronoun (me, you-singular, him, her, us, you-plural, them) before a gerund (verb+ing) A gerund is composed of a main verb with ing attached to the end of it, as in marching. The very appearance of a main verb + ing signals progressive action. Often when people talk about such progressive action, they refer to the person or thing responsible for the action, or involved in the action. It is common to hear, "I heard about Blake marching in the parade." It is also common to hear "I heard about him marching in the parade." In both sentences the wrong word precedes marching. A gerund must be preceded by either a possessive noun, as in: "I heard about Blake's marching in the parade," or by a possessive pronoun, as in "I heard about his marching in the parade." The reason that a possessive noun or possessive pronoun precedes the gerund is that the gerund is functioning as a noun. Since its root is a main verb, a gerund may be considered a verbal noun that is capable of: 1) taking an object, as in "Writing a book (object) requires discipline;" 2) being modified by an adjective, as in "Humorous (adjective) writing requires discipline;" and 3) being modified by an adverb, as in "Writing effectively (adverb) requires discipline." Use the plural possessive pronoun, their, rather than the plural nominative pronoun, they, before a noun to indicate ownership. Use the singular 1st person possessive pronoun Mine, never mines. Say an S ('S when writing) at the end of a noun to show posession, as is Bob's car.

Change the AAED sentences which follow to SAE ones by using the appropriate pronouns and 'S at the ends of nouns to show possession. Make all other changes necessary to "switch" the AAED sentences to SAE ones, in the following Exercises, based on instructions provided earlier. Afterwards, check your answers against the KEY, which follows.

Exercises to Use Possessive Pronouns and Nouns, and Make Other Changes from African American English Dialect to Standard American English

1. Gertrude ate her soup and <u>mines</u> too.

2. All the machinists went on strike to increase <u>they</u> pay.

3. Mark told all his co-workers to get they coats and leave.

4. <u>Him</u> screaming out of control was being recorded.

5. We told Bill that <u>him</u> getting fired was not Dana's fault.

6. Seven attendees at the workshop didn't get <u>they</u> prizes.

7. Trudy bank <u>give</u> her more consideration than <u>mines</u>.

8. The managers got <u>they</u> raises, but where yours and <u>mines</u>?

9. Ida witnessed <u>him</u> being pulled out of the fire.

10. Michelle Obama know she <u>be</u> wearing beautiful clothes.

11. She <u>inspiring</u> girls and women around the world.

12. <u>Him</u> wanting greater results is the sign of a true leader.

13. How the CEO's <u>borrowed</u> and <u>lost</u> 700 billion dollars?

14. In the final chapter the local citizens lost <u>they</u> mind.

15. Why those key line backers didn't play in the game?

16. When Je<u>rry</u> kids make A's in school, he <u>feel</u> so proud.

17. H<u>im</u> working all the time almost ruined his marriage.

18. Why they <u>didn't</u> see the need for marriage counseling?

19. Why Ted and Joe <u>didn't</u> download all <u>they</u> messages?

20. How you <u>recognized</u> all the students by <u>they</u> <u>name</u>?

21. Brenda picked up her purse but left <u>mines</u> in the car.

22. Seven students read <u>they</u> poems at the assembly.

23. Maribel gave both dogs <u>they</u> food at the same time.

24. Venus and Serena Williams deserve <u>they</u> honors.

25. The plumber cleared <u>they</u> drains and <u>mines</u>.

KEY

(To the Exercises to Use Possessive Pronouns and Make Other Changes from AAED to SAE)

1. Gertrude ate her soup and mine too.

2. All the machinists went on strike to increase their pay.

3. Mark told all his co-workers to get their coats and leave.

4. His screaming out of control was being recorded.

5. We told Bill that his getting fired was not Dana's fault.

6. Seven attendees at the workshop didn't get their prizes.

7. Trudy's bank gives her more consideration than mine.

8. The managers got their raises, but where are yours and mine?

9. Ida witnessed his being pulled out of the fire.

10. Michelle Obama knows she wears beautiful clothes.

11. She is inspiring girls and women around the world.

12. His wanting greater results is the sign of a true leader.

13. How did the CEO's borrow and lose 700 billion dollars?

14. In the final chapter the local citizens lost their minds.

15. Why didn't those key line backers play in the game?

16. When Jerry's kids make A's in school, he feels so proud.

17. His working all the time almost ruined his marriage.

18. Why didn't they see the need for marriage counseling?

19. Why didn't Ted and Joe download all their messages?

20. How did you recognize all the students by their names?

21. Brenda picked up her purse but left mine in the car.

22. Seven students read their poems at the assembly.

23. Maribel gave both dogs their food at the same time.

24. Venus and Serena Williams deserve their honors.

25. The plumber cleared their drains and mine.

5. Discussion: Knowing When to Use the SAE Verb Phrase <u>Will Have</u>, to replace the AAED Verb Phrase <u>Be Done</u> to Express <u>Future Perfect Tense</u>.

Those of us who speak and understand AAED, know that in the following AAED sentence, <u>two</u> <u>events</u> occur:

"By the time Bill come home, his wife <u>be</u> <u>done</u> cooked dinner."

The two events are: 1) Bill comes home and 2) his wife cooks dinner. On the following lines write these events in the <u>ORDER</u> of their occurrences:

1. _____

2. _____

(Answer: 1. his wife cooks dinner; 2. Bill comes home)

That's right. His wife cooked dinner first; later Bill came home.

Changing this African American English Dialect (AAED) sentence to one in Standard American English (SAE) results in:

"By the time Bill comes home, his wife will have cooked dinner."

This sentence expresses <u>Future Perfect Tense</u>.

What does <u>Future Perfect Tense</u> mean? Here's my quick and easy definition of each word, as I present the meaning of all three words together.

<u>Future</u> means "<u>project ahead</u>." <u>Perfect</u> means <u>finished</u> (as in a beautiful, <u>finished</u> or <u>perfect</u> piece of art); for something to reach the <u>finished</u> stage, other events had to occur in the <u>past</u> to make it so. <u>Tense</u> means <u>time</u>. Therefore, <u>Future Perfect Tense</u> means "time in which one completed event is projected to occur ahead of another event."

Example: "By the time Joey <u>walk</u> to school, his juice <u>be</u> <u>done</u> froze." This sentence reflects Future Perfect Tense in African American English Dialect (AAED). Two acts occur.

Write the two acts in *ORDER* of their occurrence below:

1. _____

2. _____

<u>Hint</u>: The event(s) mentioned <u>after</u> "Be Done" typically occur first.

(Answer: 1. his juice freezes; 2. Joey walks to school)

Changing this AAED sentence to one in SAE results in:
"By the time Joey <u>walks</u> to school, his juice <u>will have frozen</u>.

The Future Perfect Tense in SAE is formed by placing the verb phrase <u>Will</u> <u>Have</u> in front of the Past Participle Form of a Regular or Irregular Verb.

The mention of REGULAR verbs has probably peaked your interest in Learning or Re-Learning the difference between REGULAR VERBS and IRREGULAR VERBS. Very brief definitions follow, with lists of REGULAR and IRREGULAR VERBS presented <u>after</u> the Exercise on <u>Future Perfect Tense</u> and <u>before</u> the Exercise on <u>Present Perfect Tense</u>.

REGULAR VERBS

<u>Regular</u> <u>Verbs</u> tend to maintain their <u>basic</u> <u>spelling</u> or <u>form</u> throughout changes in the position (1st, 2nd, or 3rd) and number (singular or plural) of the subject, and tense (present, past, future, future perfect, or present perfect). The verb <u>wash</u> is a <u>regular</u> <u>verb</u>. It keeps its basic spelling throughout changes in verb tense, and position and number of the subject, as shown below:

Present Tense

	Singular		Plural
1st	I wash	1st	We wash
2nd	You wash	2nd	You wash
3rd	He washes	3rd	They wash
	She washes		
	It washes		

Past Tense

	Singular		Plural
1st	I washed	1st	We washed
2nd	You washed	2nd	You washed
3rd	He, she, it washed	3rd	They washed

Future Tense

	Singular		Plural
1st	I will wash	1st	We will wash
2nd	You will wash	2nd	You will wash
3rd	He, she, it will wash	3rd	They will wash

Future Perfect Tense

Singular	Plural
1st I will have washed	1st We will have washed
2nd You will have washed	2nd You will have washed
3rd He will have washed	3rd They will have washed
She will have washed	
It will have washed	

Present Perfect Tense

Singular	Plural
1st I have washed	1st We have washed
2nd You have washed	2nd You have washed
3rd He, she, it has washed	3rd They have washed

POINT #5......REMEMBER: Use the VERB PHRASE <u>WILL HAVE</u>, rather than "<u>BE DONE</u>," BEFORE THE Past Participle form of a VERB To indicate FUTURE PERFECT TENSE. Change the African American English Dialect (AAED) sentences to Standard American English (SAE) ones in the following Exercises on using <u>Future Perfect Tense</u>, and make other changes based on instructions provided earlier. Afterwards, check your answers against the KEY which follows.

Also, refer to the lists of Regular and Irregular Verbs to <u>select</u> the appropriate verb tense form.

Exercises to Use Future Perfect Tense and Make Other Changes from African American English Dialect to Standard American English.

1. By the time Joe <u>arrive</u>, they <u>be done ate</u> all the food.

2. Before Ida <u>pay</u> one bill, five more <u>be done came</u>.

3. As soon as he <u>get</u> to the meeting, it <u>be done</u> ended.

4. By the time the bus <u>come</u>, the stores <u>be done</u> closed.

5. Before the speaker <u>arrive</u>, the audience <u>be done</u> gone.

6. By the time Al <u>return</u>, his kids <u>be done growed</u> up.

7. By the time you apply for that job, it <u>be done</u> gone.

8. Once he finally <u>propose</u>, she <u>be done marry</u> another guy.

9. Before the paint <u>dry</u>, that house <u>be done</u> sold.

10. By the time Jim <u>call</u> the bankers, they <u>be done foreclose</u> on his house.

11. By the time Katy <u>pay</u> her rent, management <u>be done</u> sent her case to court.

12. Before you blink your eye, that plane <u>be done</u> took off.

13. By the time the economy <u>improve</u>, Dina be <u>done start</u> her business.

14. By the time her business <u>show</u> a profit, she <u>be</u> <u>done</u> retired.

15. By the time the kids come home, <u>they</u> Mama <u>be</u> <u>done</u> <u>fix</u> <u>they</u> snacks.

16. Before you enter the drawing, they <u>be</u> <u>done</u> <u>chose</u> a winner.

17. By the time Trudy reach the parade, her daughter and the other majorettes <u>be</u> <u>done</u> <u>finish</u> <u>they</u> <u>routine</u>.

19. By the time the search party <u>get</u> organized, the family <u>be</u> <u>done</u> found <u>they</u> dog <u>theyself</u>.

20. When Eric finally <u>arrive</u>, half the movie <u>be</u> <u>done</u> played.

21. By the time Sergeant Max get home, his family <u>be</u> <u>done</u> invited the whole town to his party.

22. Before Beth <u>notify</u> her boss that she <u>quitting</u> her job, he <u>be</u> <u>done</u> <u>got</u> <u>a</u> replacement for her.

23. By the end of the month, Holly <u>be</u> <u>done</u> <u>collected</u> more in bills than in salary.

24. By the time Amy <u>get</u> to New York, Paul <u>be</u> <u>done</u> <u>left</u>.

25. Before the firefighters arrive, the house <u>be</u> <u>done</u> burned down.

KEY

(To the Exercises to Use Future Perfect Tense and Make Other Changes from AAED to SAE.)

1. By the time Joe arrives, they will have eaten all the food.
2. Before Ida pays one bill, five more will have come.
3. As soon as he gets to the meeting, it will have ended.
4. By the time the bus comes, the stores will have closed.
5. Before the speaker arrives, the audience will have gone.
6. By the time Al returns, his kids will have grown up.
7. By the time you apply for that job, it will have gone.
8. Once he finally proposes, she will have married another guy.
9. Before the paint dries, that house will have sold.
10. By the time Jim calls the bankers, they will have foreclosed on his house.
11. By the time Katy pays her rent, management will have sent her case to court.
12. Before you blink your eye, that plane will have taken off.
13. By the time the economy improves, Dina will have started her business.
14. By the time her business shows a profit, she will have retired.
15. By the time the kids come home, their Mama will have fixed their snacks.
16. Before you enter the drawing, they will have chosen a winner.

17. By the time Trudy reaches the parade, her daughter and the other majorettes will have finished their routine.

18. Before her mailman delivers her mail, Linda will have checked her mailbox seven times.

19. By the time the search party gets organized, the family will have found their dog themselves.

20. When Eric finally arrives, half the movie will have played.

21. By the time Sergeant Max gets home, his family will have invited the whole town to his party.

22. Before Beth notifies her boss that she is quitting her job, he will have gotten a replacement for her.

23. By the end of the month, Holly will have collected more in bills than in salary.

24. By the time Amy gets to New York, Paul will have left.

25. Before the firefighters arrive, the house will have burned down.

What is PRESENT PERFECT TENSE?

Here is my simplistic definition: Present means <u>NOW</u>.

Perfect means <u>Finished</u>, and for something to be <u>Finished</u>, some steps had to be taken in the <u>Past</u>. Therefore, <u>Present</u> <u>Perfect</u> <u>Tense</u> means a Past event that is still going on NOW, as in the sentence:

>Ex. Dan <u>has kissed</u> his wife a thousand times.

This sentence means Dan kissed his wife in the past, and, no doubt, he still kisses her NOW. The present perfect tense is formed by using the Helping Verb Have or Has with the Past Participle form of the verb.

IRREGULAR VERBS

Unlike regular verbs, Irregular Verbs <u>change</u> their basic <u>form</u>, or <u>spelling</u>, especially the vowels, as the <u>tense</u>, or <u>time</u>, <u>changes</u>. The <u>forms</u> of the verb are the <u>Present Tense Form</u>, <u>Past Tense Form</u>, and <u>Past Participle Form</u>.

What is <u>Past Participle</u>? Here's my simple definition:

<u>Past</u> refers to "an event that is finished, or occurred previously."

"<u>Parti</u>" refers to "party," which consists of 2 or more; and "Ciple" refers to "follower," as in dis<u>ciple</u>, or follower of Jesus. Thus, the Past Participle Form of a verb is the spelling of a verb that <u>follows</u> another verb and usually refers to an event that occurred previously.

In the case of IRREGULAR VERBS in Standard American English (SAE) I view the Past Participle form as a "weakling," which NEVER STANDS ALONE, because it needs a "crutch" in the form of a "Helping Verb," Have, Has or Had, as shown with the Irregular Verbs, <u>See</u>, <u>Go</u>, and <u>Run</u> below.

SEE

NUMBER	POSITION	TENSE FORMS		
		Present	Past	Past Participle
	1st	I see	I saw	I have seen
	2nd	You see	You saw	You have seen
SINGULAR	3rd	He sees	He saw	He has seen
	3rd	She sees	She saw	She has seen
	3rd	It sees	It saw	It has seen
PLURAL	1st	We see	We saw	We have seen
	2nd	You see	You saw	You have seen
	3rd	They see	They saw	They have seen

GO

NUMBER	POSITION	TENSE FORMS		
		Present	Past	Past Participle
	1st	I go	I went	I have gone
	2nd	You go	You went	You have gone
SINGULAR	3rd	He goes	He went	He has gone
	3rd	She goes	She went	She has gone
	3rd	It goes	It went	It has gone
PLURAL	1st	We go	We went	We have gone
	2nd	You go	You went	You have gone
	3rd	They go	They went	They have gone

RUN

NUMBER	POSITION	TENSE FORMS		
		<u>Present</u>	<u>Past</u>	<u>Past Participle</u>
	1st	I run	I ran	I have run
	2nd	You run	You ran	You have run
SINGULAR	3rd	He runs	He ran	He has run
	3rd	She runs	She ran	She has run
	3rd	It runs	It ran	It has run
PLURAL	1st	We run	We ran	We have run
	2nd	You run	You ran	You have run
	3rd	They run	They ran	They have run

As displayed above, the Past Participle form of each Irregular Verb REQUIRES a Helper, or Helping Verb, such as <u>have</u> or <u>has</u>.

Lists of REGULAR and IRREGULAR VERBS follow. Refer to these lists as often as you need, in order to make a positive impact on others with your Spoken Word and with the written word, so that you may achieve the outcomes you desire.

REGULAR VERBS

TENSE FORMS

Present	Past	Past Participle
Answer	Answered	Answered
Argue	Argued	Argued
Ask	Asked	Asked
Attach	Attached	Attached
Attract	Attracted	Attracted
Bake	Baked	Baked
Borrow	Borrowed	Borrowed
Belch	Belched	Belched
Believe	Believed	Believed
Burn	Burned	Burned
Call	Called	Called
Carry	Carried	Carried
Climb	Climbed	Climbed
Deal	Dealt	Dealt
Dip	Dipped	Dipped
Drag	Dragged	Dragged
Dump	Dumped	Dumped
Earn	Earned	Earned
Fake	Faked	Faked

Frame	Framed	Framed
Gain	Gained	Gained
Grab	Grabbed	Grabbed
Heed	Heeded	Heeded
Help	Helped	Helped
Honor	Honored	Honored
Jump	Jumped	Jumped
Kick	Kicked	Kicked
Hang (Execution)	Hanged	Hanged
Lick	Licked	Licked
Like	Liked	Liked
Make	Made	Made
Mime	Mimed	Mimed
Nap	Napped	Napped
Occupy	Occupied	Occupied
Offer	Offered	Offered
Oil	Oiled	Oiled
Order	Ordered	Ordered
Oust	Ousted	Ousted
Owe	Owed	Owed
Park	Parked	Parked
Pass	Passed	Passed

Paste	Pasted	Pasted
Peel	Peeled	Peeled
Pick	Picked	Picked
Pump	Pumped	Pumped
Race	Raced	Raced
Raise	Raised	Raised
Sack (in football)	Sacked	Sacked
Send	Sent	Sent
Share	Shared	Shared
Tease	Teased	Teased
Test	Tested	Tested
Trust	Trusted	Trusted
Try	Tried	Tried

IRREGULAR VERBS

TENSE FORMS

<u>Present</u>	<u>Past</u>	<u>Past</u> <u>Participle</u>
Beat	Beat	Beaten
Bend	Bent	Bent
Bet	Bet	Bet
Become	Became	Become

Present	Past	Past Participle
Begin	Began	Begun
Bear	Bore	Born
Beat	Beat	Beaten
Build	Built	Built
Buy	Bought	Bought
Bleed	Bled	Bled
Blow	Blew	Blown
Break	Broke	Broken
Bring	Brought	Brought
Burst	Burst	Burst
Cast	Cast	Cast
Catch	Caught	Caught
Cling	Clung	Clung
Cut	Cut	Cut
Do	Did	Done
Drink	Drank	Drunk
Drive	Drove	Driven
Eat	Ate	Eaten
Fly	Flew	Flown
Forecast	Forecast	Forecast
Freeze	Froze	Frozen

My Fellow Americans...It's Cool to Speak Like You've Been to School
© 2009 by Bernadette Anderson, Ph.D., All Rights Reserved

Present	Past	Past Participle
Give	Gave	Given
Grow	Grew	Grown
Hang (an object)	Hung	Hung
Hear	Heard	Heard
Hide	Hid	Hidden
Hold	Held	Held
Know	Knew	Known
Lead	Led	Led
Lie	Lay	Lain
Pay	Paid	Paid
Put	Put	Put
Quit	Quit	Quit
Ride	Rode	Ridden
Ring	Rang	Rung
Rise	Rose	Risen
Say	Said	Said
See	Saw	Seen
Seek	Sought	Sought
Sew	Sewed	Sewn
Shake	Shook	Shaken
Sink	Sank	Sunk

Sit	Sat	Sat
Shine	Shone	Shone
Stand	Stood	Stood
Stink	Stank	Stunk
Think	Thought	Thought
Take	Took	Taken
Tear	Tore	Torn
Wear	Wore	Worn
Win	Won	Won

POINT #6......REMEMBER: Use the Helping Verb, Have or Has Before the Past Participle form of a VERB to indicate PRESENT PERFECT TENSE. Change the African American English Dialect (AAED) sentences to Standard American English (SAE) ones in the following Exercises based on instructions provided earlier. Check your answers against the KEY which follows. Also refer to the Lists of Regular and Irregular Verbs to select the appropriate Verb Tense form.

The Number (Singular or Plural) and Position (1st, 2nd, or 3rd) of the Subject of the sentence determine whether to use the verb Have or the verb Has before the Past Participle form of the Verb to create the Present Perfect Tense. The verb Have is used with plural subjects, including the pronouns I, you, they. The verb Has is used with singular subjects, including he, she, it.

As indicated earlier, the Present Perfect Tense refers to an act that occurred in the Past and is still going on NOW.

In African American English Dialect (AAED), the Present Perfect Tense is formed often by using the verb Done before the Past Tense form of a Verb, as in:

 Rahshad done broke another glass.

In Standard American English the sentence changes to:

 Rahshad has broken another glass.

Exercises to Use Present Perfect Tense and Make Other Changes from African American English Dialect (AAED) to Standard American English (SAE).

1. The church bell <u>done</u> <u>rang</u> every 15 minutes.

2. Sam and Darlene <u>done</u> <u>sang</u> so many songs since they been in the choir.

3. The bachelor's friends <u>done</u> <u>went</u> to a lot of trouble to show him a goodtime.

4. <u>Marsha</u> boyfriend <u>done</u> <u>shook</u> her baby and caused medical problems.

5. John and Bill <u>done</u> <u>wrote</u> fifty letters to the President.

6. Jennifer <u>done</u> <u>hid</u> her journal of love letters.

7. The judge <u>done</u> <u>took</u> a recess at the worst time.

8. What you <u>done</u> <u>heard</u> about the kids in that family?

9. Girl, what you <u>done</u> <u>did</u> to your hair?

10. Tanya <u>done</u> <u>ate</u> so much food that now she <u>tired</u>.

11. Ruth, what you <u>done</u> <u>drank</u>?

12. William <u>done</u> <u>throwed</u> another tantrum.

13. Dennis and Emily <u>done</u> <u>ran</u> so many marathons.

14. Barbara and India <u>done</u> <u>won</u> <u>they</u> races at all the track meets.

15. All the fire fighters <u>done</u> <u>been</u> in life-threatening situations.

16. Trisha <u>done</u> <u>beat</u> every other contestant for the prize.

17. The four high schools <u>done</u> <u>closed</u> <u>they</u> games to fans.

18. Fewer than three students <u>done</u> <u>earned</u> all A's this term.

19. Mike <u>done</u> <u>wore</u> a lot of colorful suits and ties.

20. Barbara wants to know if you <u>have</u> <u>began</u> to write.

21. The building supervisor <u>have</u> <u>repaired</u> the plumbing problems.

22. What you <u>done</u> <u>did</u> to my necklace?

23. Freddy <u>done</u> <u>flew</u> into the city on a private plane.

24. How much salad <u>have</u> you <u>bought</u> to the party?

25. Charlotte told me that she <u>has</u> <u>rode</u> a horse several times.

KEY

(To Exercises to Use Present Perfect Tense and Make Other Changes from AAED to SAE)

1. The church bell has rung every 15 minutes.

2. Sam and Darlene have sung so many songs since they have been in the choir.

3. The bachelor's friends have gone to a lot of trouble to show him a good time.

4. Marsha's boyfriend has shaken her baby and caused medical problems.

5. John and Bill have written fifty letters to the President.

6. Jennifer has hidden her journal of love letters.

7. The judge has taken a recess at the worst time.

8. What have you heard about the kids in that family?

9. Girl, what have you done to your hair?

10. Tanya has eaten so much food that now she is tired.

11. Ruth, What have you drunk?

12. William has thrown another tantrum.

13. Dennis and Emily have run so many marathons.

14. Barbara and India have won their races at all the track meets.

15. All the fire fighters have been in life-threatening situations.

16. Trisha has beaten every other contestant for the prize.

17. The four high schools have closed their games to fans.

18. Fewer than three students have earned all A's this term.

19. Mike has worn a lot of colorful suits and ties.

20. Barbara wants to know if you have begun to write.

21. The building supervisor has repaired the plumbing problems.

22. What have you done to my necklace?

23. Freddy has flown into the city on a private plane.

24. How much salad have you brought to the party?

25. Charlotte told me that she has ridden a horse several times.

AIN'T NOBODY...   CAIN'T NOBODY...

DON'T NOBODY...   WON'T NOBODY...

7. Discussion: African American English Dialect (AAED) speakers often use the phrases <u>Ain't Nobody</u>, <u>Cain't</u> (I have spelled can't in this way to match the pronunciation used by speakers of AAED typically) <u>Nobody</u>, <u>Don't</u> <u>Nobody</u>, and <u>Won't Nobody</u> to indicate the negative or doubtful aspect of a situation.

In Standard American English (SAE), however, the general rule of grammar tells us that use of two negatives in the Subject-Verb position results in a positive outcome. For instance, a popular sales slogan that has played on TV and radio for many years is: "Everybody doesn't like something, but nobody doesn't like Sara Lee's (bakery products)." The intent of the slogan is to convey the notion that each of us dislikes something, but there is no one who dislikes Sara Lee's. The key phrase in the slogan, "<u>Nobody Doesn't like</u>" closely resembles the AAED phrase, "Don't Nobody like." However, their meanings are different.

In AAED, a sentence that says, "Don't nobody like Sara Lee's" means "no one likes it." It is easy to see how speakers of AAED have gotten confused by the Sara Lee slogan for years. As recently as February 15, 2009, I overheard ministers and their wives in a humorous debate about the mixed meanings of the same Sara Lee slogan: "Everybody doesn't like something; but nobody doesn't like Sara Lee's."

Point #7... REMEMBER: In AAED the following negative phrases typically mean:

1. Ain't Nobody = Nobody is

> There is nobody

> Nobody has

2. Cain't (Can't) Nobody = Nobody can

(I spelled Can't as Cain't to match the pronunciation used typically in AAED)

3. Don't Nobody = Nobody does

4. Won't Nobody = Nobody will

Now change the following African American English Dialect (AAED) sentences of Negation to those in Standard American English (SAE). Check your answers against the Key, which follows.

Exercises to change the AAED sentences of Negation to SAE sentences, using "Ain't Nobody." Also make other changes from AAED to SAE based on earlier instructions. Then check your answers against those in the KEY, which follows.

1. Ain't nobody saw Ms. Brown's little white puppy.

2. Ain't nobody being paid by the comptroller now.

3. Sue can't copy the report, because ain't nobody put no paper in the printer.

4. Ain't nobody been threatening Tony.

5. Ain't nobody going to Shamicka's party.

6. Ain't nobody been inside Ms. Stewart's house.

7. Girl, ain't nobody took your make-up.

8. Ain't nobody making fun of you.

9. Ain't nobody heard the church bells in two weeks.

10. Ain't nobody bought no food to the party.

11. Ain't nobody trying to change the plans.

12. Ain't nobody did Mr. Mack's science homework.

13. Ain't nobody got no money for a movie.

14. Ain't nobody expecting more problems.

15. Ain't nobody interested in losing money.

16. Ain't nobody went fishing yet.

17. Ain't nobody asked you to come to the meeting.

18. Ain't nobody wore your blue suit.

19. Ain't nobody telling you to do what you don't want to do.

20. Ain't nobody taking care of my dog Bravo, but me.

21. Ain't nobody laid on your bed.

22. Ain't nobody going to help Mike remodel that old car.

23. Ain't nobody giving those children the training they need.

24. Ain't nobody happy about the increase in prices.

25. Ain't nobody borrowed no money from Jan.

FYI: Sometimes speakers of AAED use the word <u>bought</u> instead of <u>brought</u> as the past tense of <u>bring</u>.

KEY

(To Exercises to Change AAED Sentences of Negation to SAE)

1. Nobody saw Ms. Brown's little white puppy.
2. Nobody is being paid by the comptroller now.
3. Sue can't copy the report, because nobody has put any paper in the printer.
4. Nobody has been threatening Tony.
5. Nobody is going to Shamicka's party.
6. Nobody has been inside Ms. Stewart's house.
7. Girl, nobody has taken your make-up.
8. Nobody is making fun of you.
9. Nobody has heard the church bells in two weeks.
10. Nobody has brought any food to the party.
11. Nobody is trying to change the plans.
12. Nobody has done Mr. Mack's science homework.
13. Nobody has any money for a movie.
14. Nobody is expecting more problems.
15. Nobody is interested in losing money.
16. Nobody has gone fishing yet.
17. Nobody has asked you to come to the meeting.
18. Nobody has worn your blue suit.

19. Nobody is telling you to do what you don't want to do.

20. Nobody is taking care of my dog Bravo, but me.

21. Nobody has lain on your bed.

22. Nobody is going to help Mike remodel that old car.

23. Nobody is giving those children the training they need.

24. Nobody is happy about the increase in prices.

25. Nobody has borrowed any money from Jan.

Exercises to change the AAED sentences of Negation to SAE sentences, using "Can't Nobody." Also, make other changes based on earlier instructions. Then check your answers with those in the KEY, which follows.

1. Can't nobody pay all those other bills.

2. Can't nobody hide Alice's mistakes.

3. Why can't nobody answer the question?

4. Bob know can't nobody find his cuff links.

5. Why you don't tell Jack can't nobody win the lottery?

6. Can't nobody make Rob hang up his clothes.

7. Can't nobody trust you after your last misdeed.

8. Can't nobody send you money through the mail.

9. Can't nobody park on the east side of the street now.

10. Can't nobody peel those tiny kiwi.

11. The teacher wonder why can't nobody test higher.

12. Jackie always complain that can't nobody help her.

13. Jonathan and Ethel know can't nobody ride that horse.

14. When the <u>President</u> in town, <u>can't</u> <u>nobody</u> <u>park</u> for several blocks.

15. <u>Can't</u> <u>nobody</u> <u>match</u> your answers.

16. <u>Can't</u> <u>nobody</u> <u>sew</u> those gowns fast enough.

17. <u>Can't</u> <u>nobody</u> <u>wear</u> that size 0 skirt, but Eva.

18. <u>Can't</u> <u>nobody</u> <u>move</u> that big box of books.

19. Wendell asked, "Why <u>can't</u> <u>nobody</u> <u>sing</u> <u>Sue</u> song?"

20. Marvin <u>know</u> <u>can't</u> <u>nobody</u> <u>catch</u> his high fly.

21. Emily <u>know</u> <u>can't</u> <u>nobody</u> <u>beat</u> her at chess.

22. <u>Can't</u> <u>nobody</u> <u>drive</u> faster than 30 miles per hour.

23. Carolyn <u>say</u> <u>can't</u> <u>nobody</u> <u>cut</u> the wedding cake yet.

24. Gaby <u>know</u> <u>can't</u> <u>nobody</u> <u>care</u> for her baby like Mom.

25. <u>Can't</u> <u>nobody</u> <u>bake</u> cakes as delicious as Grace's.

KEY

(To Exercises to change the African American English Dialect sentences of Negation, which use "Can't Nobody," to those in Standard American English)

1. Nobody can pay all those other bills.

2. Nobody can hide Alice's mistakes.

3. Why can't anybody answer the question?

4. Bob knows nobody can find his cuff links.

5. Why don't you tell Jack nobody can win the lottery?

6. Nobody can make Rob hang up his clothes.

7. Nobody can trust you after your last misdeed.

8. Nobody can send you money through the mail.

9. Nobody can park on the east side of the street now.

10. Nobody can peel those tiny kiwi.

11. The teacher wonders why nobody can test higher.

12. Jackie always complains that nobody can help her.

13. Jonathan and Ethel know nobody can ride that horse.

14. When the President is in town, nobody can park for several blocks.

15. Nobody can match your answers.

16. Nobody can sew those gowns fast enough.

17. Nobody can wear that size 0 skirt, but Eva.

18. Nobody can move that big box of books.

19. Wendell asked, "Why can't anybody sing Sue's song?"

20. Marvin knows nobody can catch his high fly.

21. Emily knows nobody can beat her at chess.

22. Nobody can drive faster than 30 miles per hour.

23. Carolyn says nobody can cut the wedding cake yet.

24. Gaby knows nobody can care for her baby like Morn.

25. Nobody can bake cakes as delicious as Grace's.

Exercises to change the AAED sentences of Negation to SAE sentences, using "Don't Nobody." Also make other changes from AAED to SAE, based on earlier instructions.

Then check your answers against those in the Key, which follows.

1. Don't nobody know who sung the song.

2. Don't nobody have the answer.

3. Don't nobody earn as much money as Margaret.

4. Marion think don't nobody understand algebra like she do.

5. Don't nobody see all the kids when they help old people.

6. Don't nobody ride the Ferris wheel without screaming.

7. Don't nobody think Andrew is the best candidate.

8. Don't nobody put their personal interests first.

9. Donna ask questions that don't nobody want to hear.

10. Don't nobody eat Grandma's fruit cake.

11. Don't nobody know who drunk the last of the punch.

12. Catherine say don't nobody give enough of their time.

13. Ceasar buy houses that don't nobody else want.

14. Don't nobody believe the weather report.

15. Don't nobody grow grapes in Chicago, except the Medina family.

16. Don't nobody bring enough salad to those get-togethers.

17. Tim not coming because don't nobody offer to help him.

18. Bernard say even if don't nobody offer to help him, he coming anyway.

19. Don't nobody trust other people with they money today.

20. Don't nobody take for granted any financial help today.

21. Don't nobody expect the recession to last much longer.

22. Don't nobody think Patrick will ever retire from his job.

23. Don't nobody want the economy to fail.

24. Don't nobody argue with the instructor like Joe do.

25. Don't nobody score as high as McKnight on math tests.

KEY

(To Exercises to Change the AAED sentences of Negation, which uses "Don't Nobody," to those in SAE)

1. Nobody knows who sang the song.
2. Nobody has the answer.
3. Nobody earns as much money as Margaret.
4. Marion thinks nobody understands algebra like she does.
5. Nobody sees all the kids when they help old people.
6. Nobody rides the Ferris wheel without screaming.
7. Nobody thinks Andrew is the best candidate.
8. Nobody puts their personal interests first.
9. Donna asks questions that nobody wants to hear.
10. Nobody eats Grandma's fruit cake.
11. Nobody knows who drank the last of the punch.
12. Catherine says nobody gives enough of their time.
13. Ceasar buys houses that nobody else wants.
14. Nobody believes the weather report.
15. Nobody grows grapes in Chicago, except the Medina family.
16. Nobody brings enough salad to those get-togethers.
17. Tim is not coming because nobody offers to help him.
18. Bernard says even if nobody offers to help him, he is coming anyway.
19. Nobody trusts other people with their money today.

20. Nobody takes for granted any financial help today.

21. Nobody expects the recession to last much longer.

22. Nobody thinks Patrick will ever retire from his job.

23. Nobody wants the economy to fail.

24. Nobody argues with the instructor like Joe does.

25. Nobody scores as high as McKnight on math tests.

Exercises to change the AAED sentences of Negation to SAE sentences, using "Won't Nobody." Also make other changes from AAED to SAE, based on earlier instructions. Then check your answers against those in the key, which follows.

1. Won't nobody deal with all the problems Kim have.

2. Won't nobody borrow money from that bank.

3. Marvin think won't nobody be his friend at a new school.

4. Carl say he lies because won't nobody believe the truth.

5. Sharon jump at the chance to compete, but won't nobody else in her class do the same.

6. Derrick tell good jokes, but won't nobody laugh at them.

7. Won't nobody else vote for Millard.

8. Won't nobody be allowed to see the paintings before the judges enter the room.

9. Won't nobody frame the picture the way she want.

10. Won't nobody kick the football as far as Jonah do.

11. Won't nobody dig in the dirt to plant flower seeds the way that Sabrina do.

12. Won't nobody drink as much water as we supposed to.

13. <u>Won't</u> <u>nobody</u> <u>cut</u> the potatoes for the French fries, but everybody want to eat them.

14. <u>Won't</u> <u>nobody</u> <u>try</u> to catch a fast ball without a glove.

15. <u>Won't</u> <u>nobody</u> <u>open</u> the gifts until Trina come.

16. <u>Won't</u> <u>nobody</u> <u>drink</u> the shake until Brenda <u>drink</u> first.

17. <u>Won't</u> <u>nobody</u> <u>win</u> the race if don't nobody <u>enter</u> it.

18. <u>Won't</u> <u>nobody</u> <u>quit</u> working, even if don't nobody <u>get</u> paid.

19. <u>Won't</u> <u>nobody</u> <u>listen</u> to you, if you don't make sense.

20. <u>Won't</u> <u>nobody</u> <u>sink</u> in the water, if <u>they</u> <u>wearing</u> <u>they</u> life jackets.

21. <u>Won't</u> <u>nobody</u> <u>lead</u> the way, if the people won't follow.

22. Frank <u>think</u> <u>won't</u> <u>nobody</u> <u>vote</u> for the opposition.

23. Samuel <u>sew</u> for a living, but <u>won't</u> <u>nobody</u> <u>hire</u> him, because they don't know what he <u>do</u>.

24. <u>Won't</u> <u>nobody</u> <u>ignore</u> all the letters, e-mails, and phone calls that people sent to Washington, D.C.

25. <u>Won't</u> <u>nobody</u> <u>think</u> the <u>people</u> <u>not</u> <u>concerned</u> about the economy.

KEY

(To Exercises to change the AAED sentences of Negation, which use "Won't Nobody" to those in SAE)

1. Nobody will deal with all the problems Kim has.

2. Nobody will borrow money from that bank.

3. Marvin thinks nobody will be his friend at a new school.

4. Carl says he lies because nobody will believe the truth.

5. Sharon jumps at the chance to compete, but nobody else in her class will do the same.

6. Derrick tells good jokes, but nobody will laugh at them.

7. Nobody else will vote for Millard.

8. Nobody will be allowed to see the paintings before the judges enter the room.

9. Nobody will frame the picture the way she wants.

10. Nobody will kick the football as far as Jonah does.

11. Nobody will dig in the dirt to plant flower seeds the way that Sabrina does.

12. Nobody will drink as much water as we are supposed to.

13. Nobody will cut the potatoes for the French fries, but everybody wants to eat them.

14. Nobody will try to catch a fast ball without a glove.

15. Nobody will open the gifts until Trina comes.

16. Nobody will drink the shake until Brenda drinks first.

17. Nobody will win the race if nobody enters it.

18. Nobody will quit working, even if nobody gets paid.

19. Nobody will listen to you, if you don't make sense.

20. Nobody will sink in the water, if they are wearing their life jackets.

21. Nobody will lead the way, if the people won't follow.

22. Frank thinks nobody will vote for the opposition.

23. Samuel sews for a living, but nobody will hire him, because they don't know what he does.

24. Nobody will ignore all the letters, e-mails, and phone calls that people sent to Washington, D.C.

25. Nobody will think the people are not concerned about the economy.

PRONUNCIATION TIPS

The following pronunciation issues have been identified uniquely with speakers of African American English Dialect (AAED). As I stated at the start of this book, in business transactions, the focus should be on *what you are selling, not on any perceived mispronunciations*. I have isolated four pronunciation issues which, if mastered, should positively impact the communication outcome.

ASK

1. Many speakers of AAED pronounce this word as if it were aks, or axe. To pronounce it correctly, imagine a farmer who gets work done with the help of a donkey, or ASS. Sometimes the ASS is stubborn, so the farmer, who wears a big boot, gives it a gentle KICK, as in figure 1. You say ASS, then add the "K" sound from KICK, and you have the correct pronunciation: ASS + K, or ASSK

Say: ASS+K Repeat: ASS+K...ASS+K...ASS+K

Ask = Ass + k = "ASSK"

figure 1

ASKED

2. The PAST tense of ASK is <u>spelled</u> <u>ASKED</u>, and it is pronounced ASS+K+T. Imagine taking the sound of the final T at the end of the word PAST and add that T to the end of ASS+K to get ASS+K+T. So ASKED = ASSKT. Practice saying the three consonant sounds SKT—SKT—SKT until you feel more comfortable saying them to pronounce ASKED correctly.

Say: ASS+K+T Repeat: ASS+K+T..ASSKT...ASSKT

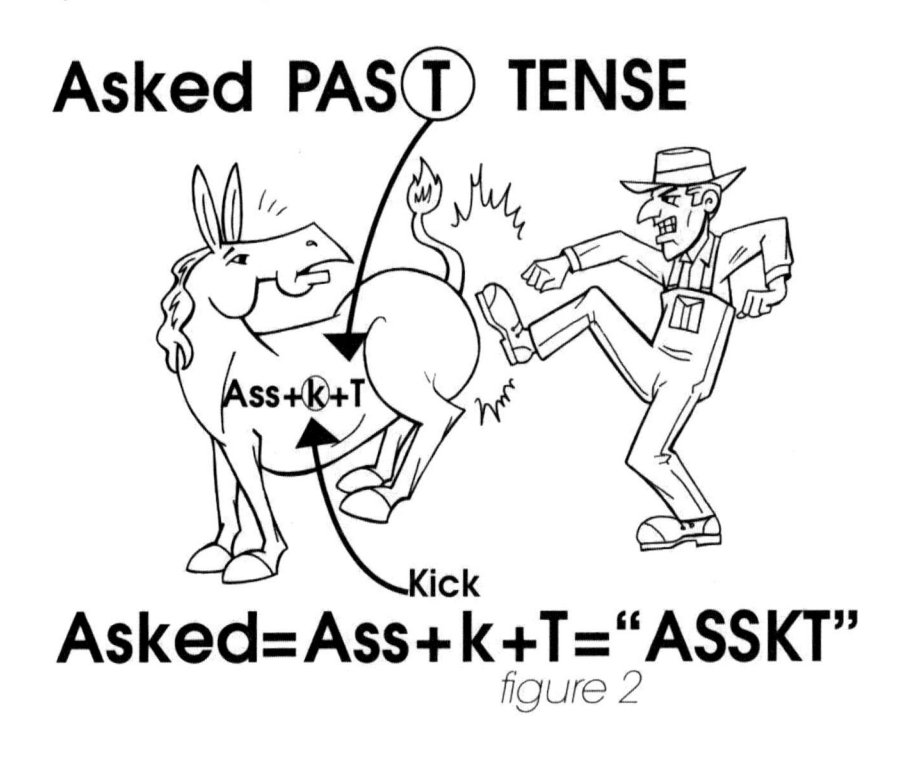

Asked PAS(T) TENSE

Ass+(k)+T

Kick

Asked=Ass+k+T="ASSKT"
figure 2

My Fellow Americans...It's Cool to Speak Like You've Been to School
© 2009 by Bernadette Anderson, Ph.D., All Rights Reserved

STR

3. Sometimes speakers of AAED pronounce the consonant blend STR as if it were SKR. For example, instead of pronouncing STREET as STREET, they say SKREET. Typically when I hear this, I have an overwhelming urge to provide pronunciation training for the speaker, whether he/she is a sales consultant, business owner, technician, etc. I do not act on that urge, however. Thus, I am pleased to share these tips here.

When it comes to saying the consonant blend STR, just say the word "STIR" (as in turning a spoon inside the batter within a bowl). Say "STIR" again. Repeat <u>STIR</u>

To pronounce the following words, say "STIR" where you see STR and then say the rest of the word. If you use this tip, you should pronounce each word correctly.

STREET   Say STIR + EET = STREET

STRONG   Say STIR + ONG = STRONG

SCR or SKR

Sometimes AAED speakers say <u>STR</u> before words starting with <u>SCR</u>, or <u>SKR</u>. To pronounce these words correctly say "SK + HER" wherever SCR, or SKR, occurs, as in: SCREAM Say SK+HER + EAM

SCRUB   Say SK + HER + UB = SCRUB

SCRATCH   Say SK + HER + ATCH = SCRATCH

The Th Sounds

4. Just when I thought I had completed this section on "Pronunciation Tips," I was reminded by a young new minister of my church to include a brief discussion about the Th sounds. As the words and passion of the minister brought most of the church congregation to a standing ovation, his saying "bofe" for both, "bref" for breath, and "mouf" for mouth brought me back to November, 1987, when I appeared as a guest on the *Oprah Winfrey Show* on the subject, "Black English Dialect: Does It Help or Hinder African Americans in the Corporate Arena?" During the show, I stated that while I was in the 4th grade in East St. Louis, Illinois, my teacher taught us about the digraph, two consonant letters representing one sound, as in the case of the Th. I told Oprah, "It was as if a light went on in my head and I chuckled because in the classroom the name is 'Smith,' but down the street from us (my family) lived the 'Smif—with an F—family!" The young, new minister demonstrated excellent skills as a public presenter, but in order to encourage his audience to listen to WHAT he is saying, rather than to HOW he is saying it, I strongly suggest that he master pronunciation of the Th sounds. There are two kinds of Th sounds, Voiceless and Voiced.

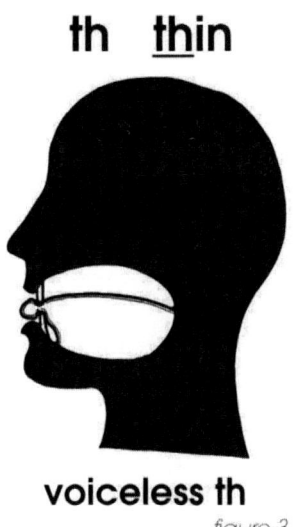

th thin

voiceless th

figure 3

Voiceless Th

Many AAED speakers say the <u>F</u> sound in place of the Voiceless <u>Th</u> sound. It is called "voiceless" because it requires <u>no vibration</u> of the vocal cords, which are muscular bands of tissue located behind the thyroid cartilage, or the "Adam's apple." The voiceless <u>Th</u> is made by placing the tongue between the teeth, raising the tongue slightly to "caress" the upper teeth, and sending air out the center of the mouth, as in Figure 3. Avoid placing your bottom lip under your upper teeth, so that you <u>do not</u> say an <u>F</u> sound in place of the voiceless <u>Th</u>. Say the following words with voiceless <u>Th</u>. Then practice saying each word in a short sentence.

<u>Initial</u> <u>Th</u>	<u>Medial</u> <u>Th</u>	<u>Final Th</u>
<u>Th</u>ink	Ba<u>th</u>room	Mou<u>th</u>
<u>Th</u>in	Bir<u>th</u>day	Bo<u>th</u>
<u>Th</u>anks	Wor<u>th</u>while	Brea<u>th</u>
<u>Th</u>orough	E<u>th</u>er	Ear<u>th</u>

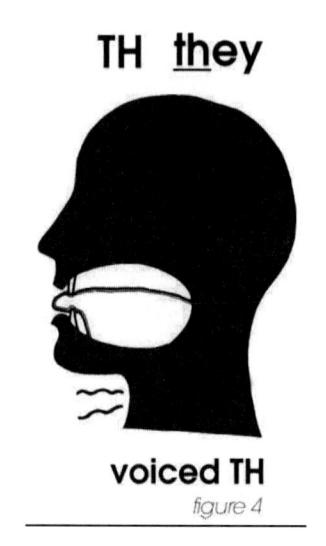

TH <u>they</u>

voiced TH

figure 4

Voiced TH

Many AAED speakers say the /d/ sound in place of the Voiced TH, especially at the beginning of words. Often AAED speakers say the /v/ sound in place of the voiced TH, especially in the medial and final positions of words. To produce the voiced TH accurately, place your tongue between your upper and lower teeth, caress the top teeth with the tongue, release air along the center of your tongue, as you "sing' a musical note. You should hear the vibration of your vocal cords. Now place the index finger and thumb of one hand at the sides of your vocal cords to feel the vibration. Figure 4 provides a drawing of the Voiced TH. Practice saying the voiced TH in the words below. Then say each word in a short sentence.

Initial Voiced TH	Medial Voiced TH	Final Voiced TH
This	Worthy	Breathe
That	Other	Loathe
These	Bother	Soothe
Those	Either	Smooth

VOICE

Breath Control: The Key

Air is the "energy food for speech." However, too many people are "undernourished speakers" because they fail to inhale before speaking and say too much on one breath. Consequently their voices sound strained and often die out toward the end. To avoid being an "undernourished speaker" follow these 8 rules.

Rule 1: Always inhale before you speak.

Rule 2: Start talking immediately after you inhale.

Rule 3: Remember to "inhale fat" (abdomen out) and "exhale flat" (abdomen in.)

Rule 4: Avoid saying a whole sentence on one breath.

Rule 5: Say only a "snatch" of an idea, or brief phrase, per breath.

Rule 6: After each "snatch" of an idea, remember to PSI, or Pause, Swallow, and Inhale.

Rule 7: Do "abdominal pulls" each time you speak.

Rule 8: To project your voice, be sure to inhale more air than usual and do "abdominal pulls" on each "snatch" of an idea you say per breath.

The Harsh Voice and How to Change It

Harshness is a subjective term used to describe a voice quality that "grates against the nerves" of listeners. Listeners perceive the harsh voice quality to be unpleasant and often characterize speakers with harsh voices as "overbearing," "belligerent," and "pugnacious," or fond of fighting. Of course, such perceptions about the speaker's personality may be totally wrong. Nevertheless, harsh voices tend to create negative impressions, not positive ones.

To change the harsh, or "gravelly" voice into one that is more resonant, pleasant or "mellow," follow the three major steps below.

Step1:   Develop good breath control by following the 8 rules described earlier.

Step 2:   Learn to relax your throat by lowering the tongue and jaw in a "yawning position." In this position keep the front of your tongue in touch with the lower gum ridge inside your mouth and lower the back of your tongue as much as possible as you inhale. Using a mirror, you should be able to see your uvula (you-view-lah), the tissue that hangs from the palate, or roof, of the mouth toward the back. Immediately before you exhale, bring your lips together, while you keep your teeth slightly apart, and hum on the /m/ sound like this: "Mmmmmm." Be aware of the "buzz," or vibration, and relaxation you feel inside your mouth. Maintain this oral "buzz" and relaxed sensation, as you practice saying the /m/ sound at the beginning of the following words in the phrases and short sentences below.

Mama mops.	Maybe Monday
Mary Martin moved.	Make mine mellow.

Step 3: Self monitor, which means: (1) listen to the sound of your voice as you say words; and (2) feel the body's responses to the way that you say words.

The Nasal Voice and How to Change It

Nasality is a subjective term used to describe a voice quality that sounds "whiny" and results from the excessive release of air near or through the nasal cavity during speech. Listeners find the nasal voice quality annoying and tend to characterize nasal speakers in such negative terms as "impatient," "insecure" and "lazy." Such terms might falsely describe the character of the speakers. Nevertheless, as in the case of the harsh voice quality, the nasal voice quality creates negative perceptions, not positive ones.

To change the nasal voice quality into one that is more resonant and clear, follow the three major steps below.

Step 1: Develop good breath control by following the 8 rules described earlier in this section on Voice.

Step 2: Practice lowering your jaw and tongue on all vowel sounds in this phrase: "H_o_t H_o_gs H_a_ve H_o_les." Place the back of your hand about 1 inch below your chin. As you say each vowel in this phrase, your chin should lower well enough to touch your hand. On each vowel you should also see your uvula, which is the tissue that hangs from the roof of your mouth. However, if you experience any discomfort in the jaw area just in front of your ears (known as the temporo-mandibular joint, or TMJ), discontinue this exercise immediately. Then concentrate more on lowering your tongue—not your jaw—as you say the vowels to enhance "oral emission," or the escape of air through the mouth, for a more resonant voice. You are encouraged to see an ear-nose-throat specialist regarding the TMJ.

Step 3: Always self monitor. Listen to the sound of your voice as your talk, and feel your body's responses. Become accustomed to how it feels inside your mouth when you are holding your tongue in a position that is low enough to reduce the nasality and modify your voice, so that it sounds resonant, richer, and powerful. Try to recreate this feeling when you are talking.

IN CONCLUSION...

My single purpose in presenting the aforementioned Exercises on changing African American English Dialect (AAED) sentences to Standard American English (SAE) is to provide the added verbal strength of versatility of the spoken word. Standard American English remains the preferred spoken code of business.

I strongly advise speakers of AAED to be bi-dialectal, able to use both SAE and AAED skillfully when the occasion requires it.

African American English Dialect is a rule-governed, effective, code of communication, which not only conveys meaning but establishes camaraderie, love, and connection. I have spoken African American English Dialect all of my life with loved ones, friends and acquaintances. Also, I have provided effective communication skills training in Standard American English to persons who primarily speak AAED and those who speak primarily SAE at various levels of corporate employment, including: CEO, management, human resources, customer service, sales, and information technology.

Years ago I created a two-cassette program titled "Speech Empowerment for African Americans." In that program I presented an inspirational history of Gullah dialect, which I describe as the "mother of Black dialect." Initially studied by the first African American linguist, Dr. Lorenzo Dow Turner, Gullah is spoken by African Americans along the coastal plains of South Carolina and Georgia. My study of Gullah, which began three decades ago, took me to the same coastal plains, ie., St. Helena Island and Daufuskie Island, SC, and climaxed with a Fulbright Hayes Scholar-based expedition to Sierra Leone, West Africa, which since 1987 has been viewed as what I have labeled the "geographic epicenter of the linguistic origins of Gullah". Around 1987 linguists arranged for twelve residents of St. Helena Island, SC, to go to Bunce Island, next to Sierra Leone, West Africa, where they met with about twelve islanders from Bunce Island. I was told that the two groups of islanders spoke Gullah with each other as clearly as if they lived in the same town, rather than in vastly separated parts of the world. I was also told that the visitors from St. Helena cried when they spoke Gullah to the islanders living on Bunce Island, because they had been brought face to face with their West African "historical, linguistic link." That link continues to be reinforced by visitors from

Sierra Leon to St. Helena Island even now. In February, 2009, a young man I met on an elevator revealed to me that he was from Sierra Leon. I asked him if he was familiar with Gullah, and he smiled and told me immediately that it is spoken by people from his native country and by African Americans on the coasts of South Carolina and Georgia. That link has been well established.

The "Link" Continues...

The economic climate today in America and across the globe is so upsetting that we must pause to see how we can link up to a power greater than the millions of jobs lost by Americans, the millions of homes lost through bank foreclosures, the billions of dollars in retirement funds and college funds lost through mismanagement and fraud. In fact the link we need is spelled out on the facades of government buildings, on the walls of our courtrooms and on every piece of money minted and printed in the USA..... "IN GOD WE TRUST." To trust means to have faith. To trust also means to have confident expectation or hope. President Obama is a man who personifies Hope for millions of people in America and abroad. But he is not God. He draws his audacity to hope from God. We too must call upon God to cause the financial storms to cease and positive economic flow to flourish. Let's get it done NOW.

ABOUT THE AUTHOR

Dr. Bernadette Anderson holds a Ph.D. in speech and language pathology and linguistics from Northwestern University. Described by Crain's Chicago Business as "Chicago's female Professor Higgins," she has learned to speak five languages, and has authored research papers, manuals, audio cassettes and CD's regarding accent/dialect modification and the improvement of articulation, pronunciation, grammar, and voice quality.

Dr. Anderson founded The Speech Excel Center, Inc., in Chicago to meet the growing need among business men and women to have refresher courses in effective speaking in order to increase their self-confidence, enhance their productivity, and heighten their professional growth.

Dr. Anderson has been interviewed on "Oprah" and on other television and radio talk shows regarding ways to improve the communication skills of business personnel.

Dr. Anderson is available to provide communication skills training to improve Speech, Voice, Grammar, and Pronunciation for Health Care Staff, Customer Service, Public Speakers, Sales and Accent Modification during workshops and one-on-one sessions. She may be reached by phone at 312-907-3634, by mail at P.O. Box 16744, Chicago, IL 60616, and by email at www.bernadettealways@att.net. Contact her today!